My MIDDLE Path

Written by
Christine H. Huynh, M.D.

Illustrated by
Margarette Ramoran

Dharma Wisdom
Dharma Wisdom, LLC

My Middle Path
***Bringing the Buddha's Teachings into Practice* series**

Dharma Wisdom, LLC
Arlington, Texas
www.DharmaWisdomDW.com

Author: Christine H. Huynh, M.D.
Illustrator: Margarette Ramoran
Designer: Darya Obraztsova

Library of Congress Control Number:
2021909308

ISBN: 978-1-951175-11-5

First Edition 2021

A path is a direction, a role in life, or a true innate nature. I can choose to go this way or that way. I can choose how I act as a daughter, a sister, or a friend. Or I can live an ordinary life with the special qualities that I was born with – the nature of love and understanding.

The Buddha was a Prince who experienced two extremes.

He saw that a life of luxury did not provide any meaning, so he tried the opposite by forgoing the comforts of life and passed out due to malnourishment.

He observed three musicians who were tuning their violins.

The first adjusted his violin strings too tight, causing them to break and unable to play any sound. The second adjusted his violin strings too loose, causing the sound to be out of tune. The third adjusted his violin strings just right and produced beautiful music.

From this insight, the Buddha
teaches the Middle Path.
It is the center and
neutral path.
It teaches me to do
things in moderation.
It teaches me to be
fair and unbiased.

The dot in the middle of the Buddha's forehead represents the Middle Path.
It is actually a white strand of hair that radiates a bright light in all directions, from Earth up to heaven and down to the underworld.
This light is the Buddha's Awakening and wisdom from deep thinking and looking inward.

The Middle Path teaches me to avoid doing too much of one thing and too little of another. I should not sleep too much or too little. I feel lazy if I sleep too much. I get tired if I sleep too little. When I sleep enough, I have the energy to study and play.

I should not overeat or starve myself. When my mom prepares my favorite food, I eat just enough to be full. I will not stuff myself as I will be uncomfortable.

If I eat too little, I will not have enough strength for my activities. I am happy when I eat in moderation.

The Middle Path
teaches me to
have balance in
my activities,
such as studying
and playing.
I also make time
to exercise and
do my chores.
This routine gives
me a healthy
body and mind.
This is my path
of being a kid.

I should follow each of my schedules for meals, exercise, play, and study throughout the day, even when I am busy.

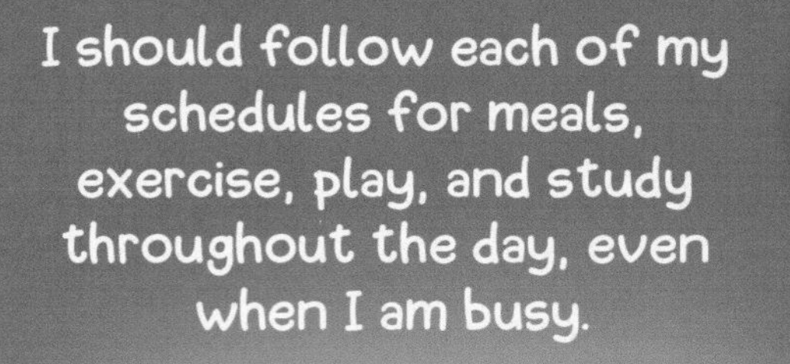

This way, I can be mindful that I live fully in each present moment.

There are many ways for me to practice the Middle Path. It is a map that provides the different routes so that I do not feel lost. Each path has its own difficulties and rewards. The main point is to know when to stop, slow down, or go in order for me to remain on the Middle Path.

Most importantly, the Middle Path teaches me to do everything right and skillfully. It has the instructions for the rule of life for me to follow. It has the power to change and improve my life – to cross over to the shore of freedom and wisdom. One skillful action directs the rest of the actions in the right path.
RIGHT
JOY
N
W
E
S

There are eight paths for me to follow in my practice. They are called the Noble Eightfold Path, the true path leading to joy and freedom.

1. Right View
2. Right Thought
3. Right Speech
4. Right Action
5. Right Job
6. Right Diligence
7. Right Mindfulness
8. Right Concentration

The first path is Right View. I practice seeing life the way it truly is rather than viewing it with my biases. I do not judge someone because of their hair or skin color. We are all the same in that we have tears that are salty and blood that is red. There are constant changes in our lives and we all depend on one another to live.

The second path is Right Thought. Having Right View leads to Right Thought. When I see things correctly, I will think properly.

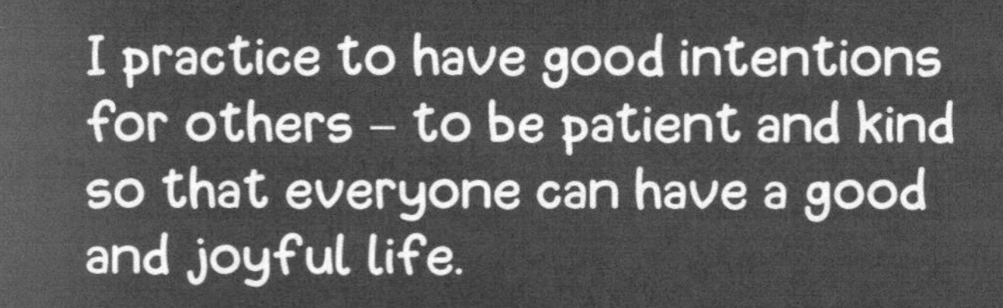

I practice to have good intentions for others – to be patient and kind so that everyone can have a good and joyful life.

The third path is Right Speech. Having Right Thoughts will lead to Right Speech. When I think of being kind, I will speak the truth with nice words to everyone. I should not tell lies when things are true, nor should I say things are true when they are actually false.

Fourth, when I see, think, and speak righteously, my actions will also be Right Actions.
Actions are what I do in my daily life. They can be what I did in the past or what I am doing right now.

The intentions of my thoughts, speech and actions are called karma. Karma determines whether I receive blessings or problems in this moment and in the future. It follows the law of Cause and Effect. Developing good intentions is important to prevent negative consequences.

There are many ways for me to act skillfully. I can adapt and be flexible in my activities. When my mom's soup tastes salty, I can add a dab of lemon juice or hot water to make it less salty. I find ways to adjust, have gratitude, and not complain so I can live freely.

I make the best out of any difficult situation. My family plans on driving a twelve-hour road trip. I cannot expect to go to the restroom whenever I want. Instead, I accept the conditions and control my water intake. This way, I can be prepared to go at the planned rest stops.

I will not be attached to the things that upset or bother me. When my friends say that my dress is not pretty, it hurts my feelings. Once my uncomfortable emotions settle, I forgive and let go. This will create peace for my heart and mind.

The fifth path is Right Job, which teaches me to act skillfully in my profession. Whatever my career choice is, I will be mindful in my work to develop thoughts, speech, and actions that provide benefit rather than harm. I want to foster virtuous karma in order to earn more blessings.

Sixth, I will commit to work with Right Diligence. I must practice my flips over and over to become a stellar gymnast. Despite many falls, I learn from my mistakes and practice steadily to perform to the best of my ability. Right Diligence is the effort that drives me to train in the other seven paths so that I may improve my character.

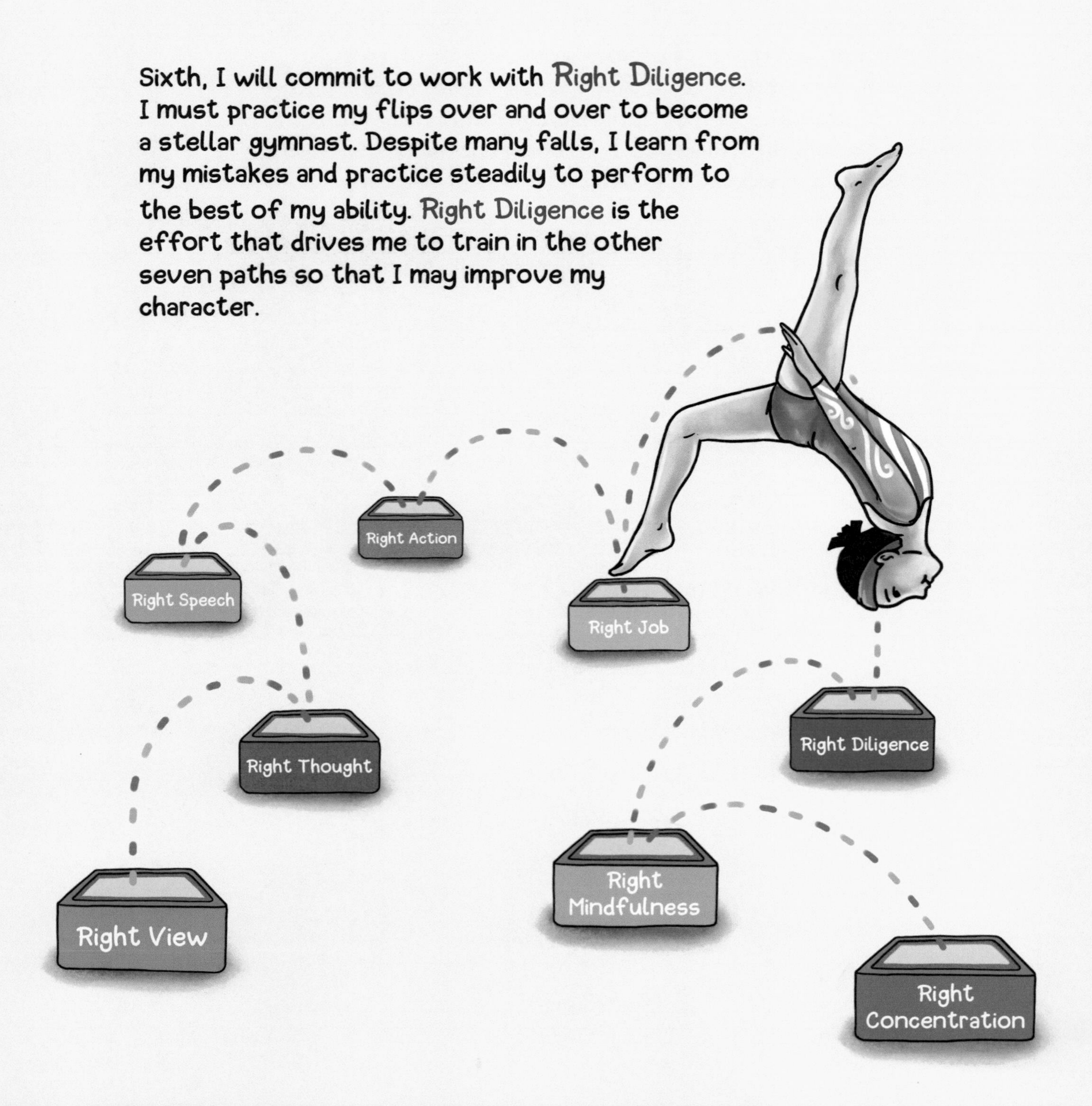

Seventh, I will practice Right Mindfulness and be open to experiencing life as it is. To practice mindfulness is to constantly be aware of my thoughts, speech, and actions in the present moment. In order to do what is right, I have to look inward and think about the situation. When I am angry, I should recognize my anger so that I do not react and express with unsightly gestures and mean words. Mindfulness is the heart of my practice.

Eighth, I will develop Right Concentration – a focused attention on a task. When I find a cell phone in the restroom, I should think of how the person who lost the phone feels. This deep awareness allows me to understand this person must be sad. My concentration gives me the wisdom to turn the phone into Lost and Found.

These Eight Paths seem a lot to remember,
but they all flow nicely together.

The key is to practice each one skillfully in order to perform
them right. I know that I am on the right path when my thoughts,
speech, and actions do not harm but benefit others and myself.
When I practice to aim to the highest level and perform
good deeds, I achieve freedom and peace for my mind.

My mind determines all my thoughts, expressions, and feelings. When I speak and act with impure thoughts, unhappiness follows like the wheels of a pulled cart rolling behind the ox.

Therefore, I must reflect and correct my faulty thoughts so that my speech and actions do not cause sorrow for myself and others.

When I speak and act with pure thoughts, happiness follows like a shadow that follows its object. My right foot takes the first step to remind me to head in the right direction. I practice this mindfully so the right actions become good habits.

This wholesome karma creates blessings for me and joy for others.

The wrong actions are far
from the right actions, just
like the sky is far
from the earth, this shore
from the other shore, the
sun from the moon, and an
unskillful person from a
skillful person. When I
have wrong views and
thoughts, I mistake
the truth to be false
and view what is false
to be true. When I have
right views and thoughts,
I know the truth is
true and a lie is false.

The Middle Path guides each of my steps towards a peaceful life. It liberates me and deters problems from arising.
It prevents me from going down the path from brightness to darkness and staying on the path of darkness. It takes me on the path from darkness to brightness and maintains my path of brightness. It directs me to a path of freedom.

The Middle Path is filled with the root and energy of goodness, awareness, truth, and compassion. It helps me to improve from bad to good, good to better, and better to best. I must practice it like the breath that my life is dependent on. My Middle Path is the Noble Eightfold Path.

Right View
Right Thought
Right Speech
Right Action
Right Job
Right Diligence
Right Mindfulness
Right Concentration

Made in United States
Troutdale, OR
12/17/2023